YOUR KNOWLEDGE HAS VALUE

- We will publish your bachelor's and
  master's thesis, essays and papers

- Your own eBook and book -
  sold worldwide in all relevant shops

- Earn money with each sale

Upload your text at www.GRIN.com
and publish for free

Patriarchy in Society and Religion. Debunking the Father of the Postmodern Evil Demon

Tarcisius Mukuka

Bibliographic information published by the German National Library:

The German National Library lists this publication in the National Bibliography; detailed bibliographic data are available on the Internet at http://dnb.dnb.de.

ISBN: 9783346340023
This book is also available as an ebook.

© GRIN Publishing GmbH
Nymphenburger Straße 86
80636 München

Print and binding: Books on Demand GmbH, Norderstedt, Germany
Printed on acid-free paper from responsible sources.

The present work has been carefully prepared. Nevertheless, authors and publishers do not incur liability for the correctness of information, notes, links and advice as well as any printing errors.

GRIN web shop: https://www.grin.com/document/983795

Patriarchy in Society and Religion
Debunking the Father of the Postmodern Evil Demon

By Dr Tarcisius Mukuka

Kwame Nkrumah University
Kabwe
Zambia

1. Introduction

Recently, my colleague from the Department of Civic Education asked me for a guest lecture on patriarchy in society and religion. I was feeling quite pleased with my lecture in which I used the term villain in reference to patriarchy. Nearly everything that was wrong in society and religion I laid at the altar of patriarchy. But the glow of self-satisfaction after puncturing patriarchy did not last long. That same evening, I came across what the American media refers to as an op-ed[1] by Cardinal Wilfrid Napier of South Africa for the *Southern Cross* entitled "Patriarchy is not the source of all evil" and immediately I became upset. Whatever the Prince of the Church intended by his op-ed, it could easily be misconstrued as letting patriarchy off the hook. This article aims at removing any such possible rehabilitation of patriarchy. I had met Cardinal Wilfrid Napier in the mid-1980s, just after my ordination to the Catholic priesthood in 1983. The venue was Lusaka at St Dominic's Major Seminary in Lusaka. After lunch, the then Secretary-General of the South African Catholic Bishops' Conference, Smangaliso Mkhatshwa introduced the South African bishops to the small group of seminary staff where I was also a visitor. Cardinal Wilfrid Napier stood out, head and shoulders above the other bishops. He was then bishop of Kokstad, long before he received the red hat from Pope John Paul II. He was suave, debonair and highly articulate. I think he was heading a delegation of South African bishops to Zambia to meet the leadership in exile of the African National Congress to facilitate its un-banning, ultimately leading to the release of Nelson Mandela from prison.

My dictionary defines the verb "to debunk" as "to expose the falseness or hollowness of (an idea or belief)" or "to reduce the inflated reputation of (someone)." I am using the verb primarily in the first sense. This article seeks "to expose the falseness or hollowness" of a millennia-old ideology. I intend to critique what I am describing as the father of the postmodern evil Demon known as patriarchy. I explore its origins going back to about four millennia ago and show that patriarchy in both religion and society is the source of the post-modern evils of domination, colonisation, and othering others, suppressing and dehumanising them, especially if these others are women. This has been the case since at least four millennia ago if not earlier. Patriarchy is not limited to domination of women. In fact, it began at the time of the shift from being hunter-gatherers to sedentary agriculturalists when gender roles begun to be defined. Men specialised in being warriors and bread winners while women focused on child rearing. They needed something to nail down their newly discovered power to dominate. They turned to patriarchy and today their invention is so steeped in religion and society that men are unlikely to relinquish it any time soon because it is in the interests of the menfolk to perpetuate it. Soon after the elf-like President Frederick Chiluba of Zambia came into power in a landslide election victory in 1991, he was heard to remark to close aides, one of whom I know, "Power is sweet."[2] I have employed two lenses to examine the evil of patriarchy: critical theory and ideology. I take cognizance of the phenomenon of patriarchy being so pernicious and widely accepted, even revered ideology that it needs to be critiqued and debunked. And so, where do I start?

2. And so, where do I start apropos the evil Demon patriarchy?

I start by introducing my two lenses: critical theory and ideology (because patriarchy is a pernicious, albeit widely accepted, even revered ideology that needs to be critiqued). I am convinced that the key to changing our patriarchal civilisation lies in debunking patriarchy and its overwhelming control over who we are, how we act, and how we think as a human race. Critical theory helps to undress and debunk the influence of patriarchy on our modern world where it has installed itself as an immoveable fixture.

First, my ideological lens. Patriarchy is the most pernicious ideology ever invented by men — I dare say it is humanity's original sin, *pace* Cardinal Wilfrid Napier — yet it is so widely accepted and revered as a male-gendered ideology that it is rarely open to challenge. My argument in this regard is that, it must be unmasked as a clear economic, cultural, political or religious ideology and not as a set of normalised relationships between the sexes and in families given to humanity by the gods. At the geopolitical and historical level, patriarchy has been the dominant driver of the values of the oppressor, the coloniser, the dominant, the victorious, and the powerful who have been, surprise, surprise, for the most part, men who prey on vulnerability.

Patriarchy as an ideology has had a pernicious effect, wreaking havoc at least over more than half of the population of the planet but as an ideology it is not always harmful, at least within a non-authoritarian society where it can prove to be democratic and positive. In fact, democracy is an ideology that most of us treasure while the values of dictatorship are almost universally reviled. We rightly loathe ideologies which suppress human freedom and patriarchy is up there with the best of them in the suppression of human rights' stakes. Suppression and dominance are almost always the values of patriarchy and yet ironically, most modern democracies are also patriarchal as the Americans learned from Donald Trump at great cost. Usually, ideology is covertly oppressive even in modern Western democracies by convincing us that education was invented to liberate our minds but in fact it was invented to colonise our minds so that we could enter the labour market for tax purposes. Unfortunately, most people idolise and fetishize democracy with no critical reflection on whether that ideal benefits their lives. Wherever it is found, and it is ubiquitous, ideology places value on rigid belief over rational thought and as soon as belief dominates an ideology, it becomes an infallible dogma that gets detached from reality and becomes repressive. Most major religions fall into this category. Even though people willingly subordinate themselves to mythical religious figures and beliefs, these values demand unbending adherence from their advocates often to the point of extremism, literally unto death. Rational logic ceases to become a mediator. That has already happened with the ideology of patriarchy. This is very well illustrated in the Catholic Church in the female ordination/non-ordination debate that has been raging literally for millennia and yet is showing no signs of abating. The official and magisterial reasons all defy all logic. It would probably

2

be easier to accept the "logic" that women cannot be ordained in the Catholic Church because they cannot pee while standing. It's that ridiculous.

Second, my critical theory lens. As Stephen Brookfield (2005) says "Critical theory views ideology as the broadly accepted set of values, beliefs, myths, explanations, and justifications that appears self-evidently true, empirically accurate, personally relevant, and morally desirable to a majority of the populace. The function of this ideology is to maintain an unjust social and political order. Ideology does this by convincing people that existing social arrangements are naturally ordained and obviously work for the good of all" (Brookfield 2005: 40–41). If patriarchy was not such a widely "accepted set of values, beliefs, myths, explanations, and justifications that appears self-evidently true, empirically accurate, personally relevant, and morally desirable to a majority of the populace," my female colleague who accepted to convert from Catholicism to Pentecostalism would not have accepted to change her faith-community to her husband's because he was the head of the house and that he had married her. After all, he had paid *lobola* (dowry or bride-price). The women who disagree with my colleague's sudden Road-to-Damascus experience — converting from Catholicism to Pentecostalism — are quick to admit that there is nothing that they can do about it. Satirically, the real reason she acquiesced to her husband's faith-community was that unlike her husband, she could not pee while standing and had no balls.

Patriarchy may be only partially biological in the sense that in the shift from being hunter-gatherers to sedentary agriculturalists, men took advantage of gender-based division of labour where men were the bread-winners and women reared children, to dominate over women. But the domination may have begun elsewhere in a militaristic context where men needed to dominate other men, enslave them and demand tribute. In times of war, even homosexual rape of the enemy was a common form of feminising and dominating the enemy. As Miranda Alison points out "Rape (even … rape of men) serves to reassert heteromasculinity" (Alison 2007: 77). In this sense domination of women through patriarchy was a win-win for men.

3. Enters a Cardinal's Anti-Patriarchy Rant

Cardinal Wilfrid Napier's "Patriarchy is not the source of all evil," which I mentioned in my introduction begins with what feels like a defence of patriarchy tinged with sarcasm. "Just look at what man is being subjected to today. At every turn he is being told he is responsible for everything that is wrong in society, from exclusive language to male domination to the oppression of woman by giving her too many children to forcing her to stay at home to look after his brood to denying her the opportunity to lead the family and indeed society to keeping her out of key decision-making processes affecting the nation and country, and so on. At every turn, he is being told he is nothing but trouble. Of course, this is not the fault of every single man, but of manhood as such, because they and they alone invented patriarchy and have forced it on woman from day one! It's no wonder that modern man is but a pale shadow of the magnificent creature, who after his creation by God together with woman was approved of and admired in the words: "And God saw all that he had created and indeed it was very good" (cf. Gen 1.31).[3] I hate to break it to the Cardinal, yes, "At every turn [male *homo sapiens*] is responsible for everything that is wrong in society, from exclusive language to male domination to the oppression of woman by giving her too many children to forcing her to stay

3

at home to look after his brood to denying her the opportunity to lead the family and indeed society to keeping her out of key decision-making processes affecting the nation and country, and so on." This has been achieved at the individual, institutional and cultural levels. Cardinal Wilfrid Napier just took the words right out of my mouth.

After some expected pious platitudes on original sin, which I suspect he understands ontologically, Cardinal Wilfrid Napier then comes out all guns blazing. "But when it comes to male-female relations, the current predominant form of blaming is patriarchy. This nebulous, ill-defined concept is used to paint man as utterly soulless, heartless, all out to dominate, to brutalise and to exploit woman, at every opportunity and in every possible way. It is assumed to be true, and to be man's evil design to make life as easy and carefree for himself as possible. All responsibility has been shifted over to woman, while he enjoys the life of Riley! Something has to be done to restore the order of things. So, patriarchy has to be eradicated once and for all. A woman must be equal to man in everything and in every way possible! That's the bottom line!"[4] There is nothing "ill-defined" about patriarchy except on his world. Yes, it is "man's evil design to make life as easy and carefree for himself as possible." Once again, he just snatched the words right out of my mouth.

Of course, Cardinal Wilfrid Napier does not believe for one minute that "patriarchy has to be eradicated once and for all." He does not believe, as I do, that patriarchy is the villain or the root of all evil, if not Satan incarnate. His take is that it is all down to original sin. "The truth revealed by God is that although man and woman were created in his image and likeness, that image and likeness was tarnished and even destroyed by their original sin of disobedience, which they committed by eating of the forbidden fruit. That act of disobedience destroyed not only their relationship of friendship and familiarity with God, but also the harmony and peace of their life together. From that moment forward everything between man and woman was, and continues to be, fraught with misunderstanding, mistrust, tension and conflict."[5] I think that is simplistic, if not naïve. It sounds as if this well-educated clergyman understands that whole eating of the forbidden malarkey literary. It is a metaphor your eminence.

4. Meet the Father of the Postmodern Evil Demon: What's Patriarchy?

I got so carried away with Cardinal Wilfrid Napier's letting patriarchy off the hook that I forgot to define what we were talking about. First, let's meet postmodernism before we meet its evil demon. "Postmodernism" is a fluid term. It is so frequently used yet so little understood that its very lack of stability and fixity could be said to warrant the notion of a condition we find ourselves in known by the catch-all postmodern. In his book, *The Postmodern Condition* (1979), Jean-François Lyotard suggests the following definition of the word. Postmodernism "designates the state of our culture following the transformations which, since the end of the nineteenth century, have altered the game rules for science, literature, and the arts" (Lyotard 1979: xxiii). I know, not exactly crystal clear. Part of the transformation was a shift from ontological epistemology to constructivist epistemology.

Second, let's meet the evil or Satan. Patriarchy is a socio-economic, political, cultural and religious hydra in which men hold power and predominate in roles of social, economic and cultural leadership. This form of abuse spills into claiming moral authority, social privilege and control of property where they have no warrant. Some patriarchal societies are also patrilineal, meaning that property and title are inherited by the male lineage. As a young boy growing up just after the independence of Zambia, I often wondered what the significance of the nomenclature of most post-colonial companies such as Thatcher & Sons, the first company to run a public bus service, later giving us the vernacular word for a bus, *Sacha* (a corruption of Thatcher). It's the "sons" that got me thinking whether the poor sod who owned the company had no daughters. The answer was simple, patriarchy. Patriarchy was associated with a set of ideas, a patriarchal ideology that acted to explain and justify dominance as if this how things were right from the beginning of creation. In fact, in the evolution of *homo sapiens*, patriarchy is a late arrival into our civilisation. It was not ever thus. Patriarchy may be as young as four thousand years — at least according to Gerda Lerner's 1986 history classic, *The Creation of Patriarchy* — and yet we act as if it was always written on tablets of stone since the foundation of the world. Sociologists hold varied opinions on whether patriarchy is a social product or an outcome of innate differences between the sexes. Historically, patriarchy has manifested itself in the social, legal, political, religious, and economic organization of a range of different cultures. Even if not explicitly defined to be such by most constitutions and laws, most contemporary societies are, in practice, patriarchal. If that is not humanity's original sin, the I don't know what is. In an interview with Jeffrey Mishlove on "Thinking Aloud," Gerda Lerner described her work on the subject of patriarchy as follows.

> Other groups that were subordinated in history — peasants, slaves, colonials, any kind of group, ethnic minorities — all of those groups knew very quickly that they were subordinated, and they developed theories about their liberation, about their rights as human beings, about what kind of struggle to conduct in order to emancipate themselves. But women did not, and so that was the question that I really wanted to explore. And in order to understand it I had to understand really whether patriarchy was, as most of us have been taught, a natural, almost God-given condition, or whether it was a human invention coming out of a specific historic period. Well, in *The Creation of Patriarchy* I think I show that it was indeed a human invention; it was created by human beings, it was created by men and women, at a certain given point in the historical development of the human race. It was probably appropriate as a solution for the problems of that time, which was the Bronze Age, but it's no longer appropriate, all right? And the reason we find it so hard, and we have found it so hard, to understand it and to combat it, is that it was institutionalised before Western civilisation really, as we know it, was, so to speak, invented, and the process of creating patriarchy was really well completed by the time that the idea systems of Western civilisation were formed.[6]

Robert Bahlieda is therefore able to conclude that "patriarchy is the primary and oldest group-think ideology of humankind upon which all other ideologies are premised and from which all other ideologies arise. It is interwoven with culture, gender, economics, religion, education, leadership, and power. These elements are the lifeblood of all our global social institutions. Patriarchy simultaneously coexists within these bodies while also creating their complexity. It has not taken control of society overnight but through a glacially slow evolution throughout human history in which generation after generation has been socialized into its ideologically restrictive belief system and relationships" (Bahlieda 2015: 22).

5. What's in a Name?

I dare not cite the famous quote from *Romeo and Juliet* in full, lest I give the evil demon known as patriarchy a positive spin it does not deserve. Etymologically, the word patriarchy literally means "the rule of the father" and comes from the Greek word πατριάρχης (*patriarkhēs*), father or chief of a race" which is a compound of πατριά (*patria*), "lineage, descent" (from πατήρ *patēr*, meaning, father) and ἀρχή (*arkhē*), "domination, authority, sovereignty." Historically, the term patriarchy has been used to refer to autocratic rule by the male head of a family, what the Romans referred to as the *Paterfamilias*. However, since the late 20th century it has also been used to refer to social, cultural, economic and political systems in which power is primarily held by adult men and sometimes not so adult such as boy-kings like Tutankhamun who took the throne at eight or nine years of age under the unprecedented viziership of his eventual successor. This concept of patriarchy is particularly beloved by writers associated with second-wave feminism such as Kate Millett, author of *Sexual Politics* (1970 [2016]). These writers seek to use an understanding of patriarchal social relations to liberate women from male domination, *pace* once more Cardinal Wilfrid Napier. This concept of patriarchy was developed to explain male dominance as a social, rather than biological, phenomenon as most men would have us believe, captured by my satirical metaphor of men peeing while standing hypothesis (Mukuka 2021). Yet the link with biology refuses to go away completely. This biological link may be as silly as, men are stronger and more powerful than women because men can pee while standing and have balls, as I have satirised elsewhere (Mukuka 2021)[7] while women can only pee seating down.

6. But Where does the Father of the Postmodern Evil Demon come from?

There are two simple answers to this which are mutually exclusive. The first answer, preferred by men is that patriarchy is biological given to us by nature, by god or the gods and if you are such a male and you happen to be of a conservative Christian ilk you add a reason from the Bible or divine revelation. You add, erroneously, if I might remind you, that the male was created first to accentuate your primacy over the woman. The woman was surgically engineered from the rib of a man and therefore she is your inferior by-product. The woman was then passed on to you, the man as a helper or a maid. Should some *ignoramus* object that this is from the Old Testament, you are happy to throw the letter to the Ephesians (Eph 5.21–33) in his face to the effect that St Paul tells the woman to be submissive to the man because the man is the head of the house. Sadly, this too is an abuse of the text as I have argued in "The Man as Head of the House: The Peeing while Standing Hypothesis" (Mukuka 2021). There I argue that the source of the misconception that the man is the head of the house is based on a misunderstanding of the use of analogy or metaphor in the Bible. Most patriarchal Neanderthal readers will be shocked to learn that Eph 5. 21–24 does not even say that the man is the head of the house. The head of the house is Jesus Christ because the Christian family is a domestic Church, the bride of Jesus Christ, the bride. By claiming to be the head of the house, the man is usurping powers that do not belong to him. Ettore Ferrari refers to this male despotism as "an idolatry of maleness,"[8] Although referring to the absurdity of the exclusion of women from Holy Orders in the Catholic Church, what Ettore Ferrari says is equally applicable to the claim of the man to be head of the house. "Maleness, in other words, is given a significant weighting over all other social and cultural differences, including femaleness. In this sense, this belief represents an idolatry of maleness — an exalting of male over female, despite the inclusive impetus of baptism and despite the fact that, in creation, women as well as men are made equally in God's image."[9] This is what the text says, "[21] Be subject to one another out of reverence for Christ. [22] Wives, be subject to your husbands as you are to the Lord. [23] For the husband is the head of the wife just as Christ is the head of the Church, the body of which he is the Saviour. [24] Just as the Church is subject to Christ, so also wives ought to be, in everything, to their husbands" (*NRSV*). I argue that the man is described as *kephalē* of the woman, whether understood as head or source of the wife, not to tell us who is boss but to use the human experience of spousal love as an analogy for the love between Jesus Christ (the husband) and the Church (the wife). Once the analogy is understood, it is no longer about husband and wife but about the Church's relationship with her spouse Jesus Christ. This point is made clear at the conclusion of the chapter where St Paul spells it out in black and white, "[32] This is a great mystery, and I am applying it to Christ and the Church. [33] Each of you, however, should love his wife as himself, and a wife should respect her husband" (Eph 5. 5. 32–33 *NRSV*).

The second answer to the question, "Where does the father of the postmodern evil demon come from?" comes from the feminist camp. The best representative of this camp is Gerda Lerner in her book, *The Creation of Patriarchy* (1986). As Gail Omvedt's string of questions at the head of her review of *The Creation of Patriarchy*, the book provides answers to the following questions, "What is the origin of women's subordination? Has it existed since the beginning of human society? Since the origin of private property? Of the state? Of agriculture? When did men gain power?" (Omvedt 1987: 70). Gerda Lerner's *The Creation of Patriarchy* deals with the rise of the state and the question of origins. She uses archaeological and written evidence to explore the Mesopotamian, Sumerian, Babylonian, Akkadian worlds (where our civilisation began in the Middle East) and finally Hebrew cultures covering the period 3500 BCE to 500 BCE, some half a century before the *Anno Domini* era. The result is hitherto new evidence about the origins of patriarchy and its connection with the processes of state and class formation. In five words, patriarchy was invented by men. Forget God or the gods. The Bible was a product of that civilisation and therefore not surprisingly paints a patriarchal world view. After all, the human authors of the Bible were all men, as was the Quran for that matter. Briefly, Gerda Lerner argues persuasively that biological differences, mainly to do with child rearing, were determinant for the earliest gender division of labour. Once agriculture began, men seized opportunity to take control because of their evolutionary strength. Elders in society began to dominate over the young and men began to dominate over women in a lineage society that included patrilineal kinship and the exchange of women. A woman was now principally an incubator and a chattel. According to Gerda Lerner, this puts the origin of our evil demon patriarchy in the 8000–3000 BCE period, when early agriculture began to yield a surplus and the beginnings of militarisation helped males to seize control of the surplus and the main producers of labour power, women. "The archaic state in the Ancient Near East," Gerda Lerner

7

explains, emerged "from the twin roots of men's sexual dominance over women and the exploitation by some men of others. From its inception, the archaic state was organised in such a way that the dependence of male family heads on the king or state bureaucracy was compensated for by their dominance over their families" (Lerner 1986: 266). Perhaps it is best to let Gerda Lerner speak for herself in propositions that sum up the origin of patriarchy, cited here at length.

a) The appropriation by men of women's sexual and reproductive capacity occurred prior to the formation of private property and class society. Its commodification lies, in fact, at the foundation of private property.

b) The archaic states were organised in the form of patriarchy; thus, from its inception the state had an essential interest in the maintenance of the patriarchal family.

c) Men learned to institute dominance and hierarchy over other people by their earlier practice of dominance over the women of their own group. This found expression in the institutionalisation of slavery, which began with the enslavement of women of the conquered group.

d) Women's sexual subordination was institutionalised in the earliest law codes and enforced by the full power of the state. Women's co-operation in the system was secured by various means: force, economic dependence on the male head of the family, class privileges bestowed upon conforming and dependent women of the upper classes, and the artificially created division of women into respectable and not-respectable women.

e) Class for men was and is based on their relationship to the means of production: those who owned the means of production could dominate those who did not. For women, sex is mediated through their sexual ties to a man, who then gives them access to material resources. The division of women into "respectable" (that is, attached to one man) and "non-respectable" (that is not attached to one man or free of all men) is institutionalised in laws pertaining to the veiling of women.

f) Long after women are sexually and economically subordinated to men, they still play active and respected roles in mediating between humans and gods as priestesses, seers, diviners and healers. Metaphysical female power, especially the power to give life, is worshipped by men and women in the form of powerful goddesses long after women are subordinated to men in most aspects of their lives on earth.

g) The dethroning of the powerful goddesses and their replacement by a dominant male god occur in most Near Eastern societies following the establishment of a strong and imperialistic kingship. Gradually the function of controlling fertility, formerly entirely held by the goddesses, is symbolised through the symbolic or actual marrying of the male god or God-King with the Goddess or her priestess. Finally, sexuality (eroticism) and procreativity are split in the emergence of separate goddesses for each function, and the Mother-Goddess is transformed into the wife/consort of the chief male God.

h) The emergence of Hebrew monotheism takes the form of an attack on the wide spread cults of the various fertility goddesses. In the writing of the Book of Genesis, creativity and procreativity are ascribed to an all-powerful God, whose epitaphs of "Lord" and "King" establish him as a male god, and female sexuality other than for procreative purposes becomes associated with sin and evil (Lerner 1986: 9–10).

That, in a nutshell, is how the evil demon patriarchy came about and both men and women have conspired to write it in stone, making any changes almost well-nigh impossible as my professional colleague with a Master's degree showed me as we were discussing her proposal for her doctoral research. I am totally in agreement with Gerda Lerner's propositions except for the last one which interprets patriarchy in the Hebrew Bible. At the risk of hubris, I probably know a bit more about the Hebrew Bible than Gerda Lerner with my humble MPhil in Biblical Sciences which included biblical archaeology at the Hebrew University in Jerusalem and a doctorate in biblical hermeneutics in which the text she refers to in the last proposition makes a cameo. She is right, though, that the Hebrew Bible represents a stage in the masculinisation of deity which fed into patriarchy.

I think Gerda lerner could have been more nuanced regarding "female sexuality" being reserved "for procreative purposes" and becoming "associated with sin and evil." It is not that unequivocal. For a start, there is a positive spin in the creation of man and woman right at the beginning, "So God created humankind in his image, in the image of God he created them; male and female he created them" (Gen 1.27 *NRSV*). Sin does not enter the picture until two chapters later and even there, there is no mention of sex. The three consequences of sin are alienation of labour, pain in child labour, the continued ding-dong between good and evil and yes, *touché* Gerda Lerner, male domination.

At the end of the metaphorical sixth day of creation, "God saw everything that he had made [including sexuality and gender], and indeed, it was very good. And there was evening and there was morning, the sixth day" (Gen 1.31 *NRSV*). In a recognition of the importance of female gender, "Then the Lord God said, 'It is not good that the man should be alone; I will make him a helper as his partner'" (Gen 2.18 *NRSV*). Perhaps, "helper" should have been translated as "complement." When God creates a woman, man for the first time breaks into ecstatic poetry, "This at last is bone of my bones and flesh of my flesh; this one shall be called Woman, for out of Man this one was taken" (Gen 2.23 *NRSV*). This was the scene until sin, through patriarchy entered the world. So, you can't completely blame the Bible for patriarchy. Th buck stops at patriarchy. The evil demon patriarchy had already been installed in the Ancient Near East long before the Hebrew Bible was written, or at least edited around 650 BCE.

7. Patriarchy in Society

The manifestations of patriarchy in society are literary myriad. But first, it is important to distinguish three forms of patriarchy: individual, institutional or systemic and cultural as does the Anti-Oppression Resource and Training Alliance [AORTA]. They gives the following manifestations of individual patriarchy, admittedly most of the examples come from the West or the Middle-East:

i. Street harassment of women and feminine-presenting people [such as trans-gender people.
ii. Using words like "bitch," "girls," "pussy," in a way that equates femininity with weakness or wrongness.
iii. Misogynist jokes ("dumb blonds", rape jokes, "my wife is a nag", etc.)
iv. A feminine person being made to feel afraid of wearing feminine clothes or showing skin, and instead feeling a need to wear more masculine clothes in order to gain respect or avoid harassment.
v. A masculine person interrupting a feminine person while they are speaking.
vi. Parents or teachers policing children's gender expression: "boys don't cry," "girls don't get dirty," "toughen up," "don't play with that truck, doll, etc." (This is often based on fear/wanting children to be safe from bullying and attacks).[10]

Institutions are neutral by nature but they get twisted as they go along depending on the ideology of the hegemonic powers. Institutions include things like: the government, corporations, non-governmental organisations, faith-based organisations, families, and places of worship. Patriarchy at this level refers to the ways that institutions maintain male domination over women. Examples of this can be conscious: intentional policies, laws, actions (which is what we often think about). Also included in the institutional level are the results of the default patterns and ways that institutions operate. These are usually unconscious, and are no less powerful or impactful. They include the following manifestations:

i. Bathrooms are gender-segregated in most buildings, forcing trans-gender or gender non-conforming people to choose which one to use, and putting them at risk of harassment, violence, and assault.
ii. Women still earn approximately 79 cents to men's 1 dollar (Black women, on average, earn 60 cents to every white man's 1 dollar, based on census data).
iii. Caretaking work, most often relegated to women, is under-recognised and undervalued. This includes caring for children, elders, and the household as well as workplace roles such as taking notes in meetings, recognising and appreciating others' labour, clean up, etc.
iv. Many school dress codes enforce gender-specific policies that place the blame on girls for "distracting" other students by showing arms, shoulders, knees, midriffs, etc.
v. Masculine voices dominating in meetings in terms of time, volume, higher esteem.
vi. Women and trans-gender people often do unrecognised, undervalued work, taking notes in meetings, taking care of others, getting food and drinks.

vii.   Globally, men dominate well-esteemed and well-paid industries (science, political leaderships) and in the U.S. women earn approximately 75% of what men earn in a lifetime.[11]

8. Patriarchy in Religion

Almost all organised religions further and sometimes thrive on the idea of male superiority simply because they can pee while standing. Such religions characterise women as physically, mentally, emotionally and sexually inferior to men. There is even a passage in 1 Peter which paints women as the weaker sex, despite the ambiguity of the text. "Husbands, in the same way, show consideration for your wives in your life together, paying honour to the woman as the weaker sex, since they too are also heirs of the gracious gift of life — so that nothing may hinder your prayers" (1 Peter 3.7 *NRSV*).

Men have welcomed patriarchy like manna from heaven, arrogating to themselves special rights and privileges on account of being "naturally" superior to their female counterparts or so they would like to make us believe and so far have succeeded. Most of this belief is as a result of a subconscious inferiority complex. For example, in Islam, the right to unilaterally divorce one's spouse is enjoyed only by men. The logic behind this is that female nature is wanting in rationality and self-control, despite evidence to the contrary.

The tendency of "patronising" and "guiding" is not restricted to Islam. Almost all religions and their holy Writs advocate domination of females by males and present the same as something that is actually beneficial for women. Despite my positive evaluation of the Hebrew Bible vis-à-vis women above, the book of Genesis is guilty of blatant sexism and patriarchy when God tells the woman, "I will greatly increase your pangs in childbearing; in pain you shall bring forth children, yet your desire shall be for your husband, and he shall rule over you" (Gen 3.16 *NRSV*). More than two millennia have passed since those words were edited and both men and women have bought them, hook, line and sinker.

In Hinduism, the practice of *Sati*, or self-immolation by widows on the funeral-pyres of their husbands, thrived for centuries because it was rooted in the belief of the futility of a woman's existence in whom she was embedded without whom her life is meaningless. Unfortunately, the accompanying social conditions, a handiwork of religious rules and regulations, only served to lend credence to this evil. Though having no direct reference or endorsement in the Hindu Scriptures, *Sati* was largely practised among certain Hindu communities because it conformed to the general idea of an "ideal" wife as epitomised by Goddess *Sati* who immolated herself because she was unable to bear the humiliation heaped on her husband, Lord Shiva, by her father.

In almost all organised religions, restrictions exist over a woman's choices over her body, sexuality, lifestyle, clothes, and just about everything. Sexuality and reproductive rights are especially problem-area with regard to women. Almost all religions advocate "sexual exclusivity" for women while exonerating men from the same obligation. *Hijab*, *Niqab*, veils, *sindoor* and *mangalsutra* are all religiously-endorsed tools for showcasing and implying "sexual exclusivity" of women as the chattel of her husband.

Whatever reasons are cited for the use of these "markers" of sexual exclusivity and whatever arguments are given in support of them, it is pretty obvious that the bottom line is: to rein-in and "protect" the sexuality of women. It is justified that women dress modestly in most cultures but the same is never required of men. Some modern fashions, in fact, encourage tight trousers so that the shape of the member can be visible to parade his masculinity. If a woman dressed in a skimpy dress or short skirt, she would be described as cheap. Why, otherwise, in an institution having two people as partners, would only one partner be expected to "showcase" their marital status and, hence, sexual exclusivity? The use of *hijab*, *niqab* and other forms of veils to "protect" women from the male gaze and possible sexual "misadventures" is well-documented. Everyone knows whose rights are being protected: the husband's. Most religious texts openly discriminate between males and females when it comes to expression of sexuality and sexual desires.

What is alarming is how deeply religiously-endorsed patriarchy is steeped into the common psyche and behaviour of the worshipper because the Bible or Quran tells me so. Incidentally, the Supreme or High God in most religions is always envisioned as male and macho. *Marduk*, the Babylonian god even murdered her sister *Tiamat* as raw material for creating the earth. Scriptures are mostly written and interpreted by men who tweak and translate them to suit their own vision of the desirable social-order and preferable gender-dynamics designed to protect the interests of the man. Religious organisations are dominated by men and are largely off-limits for women in terms of leadership and decision-making although it is commonly acknowledged that women tend to be more religiously and morally inclined and possess the qualities needed for the discharge of duties that these organisations entail. In fact, generally, women may be said to be more intelligent than men. That is why women are better at multi-tasking. Men only excel at having sex on the brain nearly all the time.

Catholicism forbids women from becoming priests simply because a priest stands *in persona Christi* [in the person of Christ] because it is important that the priest be male because Jesus Christ was male. Never mind that the point of the incarnation (cf. John 1.14) was about Jesus becoming human. Even the Nicene Creed makes the same point, which the *Catechism of the Catholic Church* gets horribly wrong. The Nicene Creed says, τὸν δι' ἡμᾶς τοὺς ἀνθρώπους καὶ διὰ τὴν ἡμετέραν σωτηρίαν κατελθόντα καὶ σαρκωθέντα καὶ ἐνανθρωπήσαντα [For us human beings and for the sake of our salvation he came down and took flesh and became human]. John Fotopoulos and Aristotle Papanikolaou, as the names tell you are Greek. They argue that "It [the translation] is unjustifiable because 'men' is not the most accurate translation for the word ἀνθρώπους in contemporary English. Rather, translating ἀνθρώπους as 'men' can be viewed, at best, as an expression of outdated English usage and, at worst, as an expression of gender exclusive English translation. There is no good reason to use outdated English in a new translation of the Creed or to use a gender exclusive English term when ἀνθρώπους is meant to be inclusive. The word ἄνθρωπος is the generic term for a human being in ancient Greek, while there are other terms for "man" and "woman." In ancient Greek, the term for "man" is ἀνήρ and the term for "woman" is γυνή. The phrase δι' ἡμᾶς τοὺς ἀνθρώπους ("for us humans") in the Creed — instead of δι' ἡμᾶς τοὺς ἄνδρας ("for us men") — was obviously deliberate and inclusive insofar as it conveys that the Son of God came down from heaven for all humans, not just for males. In fact, the formulation τὸν δι' ἡμᾶς τοὺς ἀνθρώπους καὶ διὰ τὴν ἡμετέραν σωτηρίαν κατελθόντα ἐκ τῶν οὐρανῶν is meant to correspond with the next clause — καὶ σαρκωθέντα ἐκ Πνεύματος Ἁγίου καὶ Μαρίας τῆς παρθένου, καὶ ἐνανθρωπήσαντα. It is the Son of God who came down from heaven "for us humans (δι' ἡμᾶς τοὺς ἀνθρώπους" and "became human (καὶ ἐνανθρωπήσαντα)."[12]

In logic-defying reasoning, Catholics go on to argue that, as per Tradition, since Jesus selected only male apostles and did not ordain women, the inclusion of women is not considered desirable. Hence the exclusion of women from the Catholic priesthood continues. In Islam, women cannot lead prayers as 'imams' in mosques and in mixed gatherings. Women can lead prayers in women-only gatherings as is the general pattern in South Asia, thereby, conforming to the policy of segregation as advocated by the Holy Scriptures.

Women priests in Hindu temples are extremely rare because women are 'biologically' unfit for the job as menstruating women are deemed impure and unfit for 'sacred' duties pertaining to God. This is also the reason why women are denied entry to places of worship when they are menstruating. The fear of divine reprisal prevents women from demanding equal rights in religious affairs and a more egalitarian social-order. They simply accept this discrimination as 'natural' and 'god-ordained'.

What is ironic is that most organised religions of today were originally not discriminatory to begin with, especially during the worship of earth mother-godess. In fact many scholars contend that religions were not patriarchal in the early stages of organised life. It is believed that early religions, or more appropriately worship, centred on goddesses during prehistoric times. It is believed that prehistoric societies and belief systems were matriarchal, as evident from their feminine-themed iconography.

9. Conclusion

This article has examined the origins of the father of the postmodern evil Demon known as patriarchy. I argue that patriarchy in both religion and society is the source of the post-modern evils of domination, colonisation, othering others, suppressing them, especially if these others are women. This has been the case since at least four millennia ago if not earlier. Patriarchy is not limited to domination of women. In fact, it began at the time of the shift from being hunter-gatherers to sedentary agriculturalists when gender roles begun to be defined. Men became warriors and bread winners while women focused on child rearing. Patriarchy is now so steeped in religion and society that men are unlikely to relinquish it any time soon because it is in the interests of the menfolk to perpetuate it. I have employed two lenses to examine the evil of patriarchy: critical theory and ideology.

I take cognizance of the phenomenon of patriarchy being so pernicious and widely accepted, even revered ideology that it needs to be critiqued and debunked. It is not a sacred cow. I am convinced that the key to changing our patriarchal civilisation lies in debunking patriarchy and calling it out for what it is, its overwhelming control over who we are, how we act, and how we think as a human civilisation and how it hampers global development. We need to teach future generations to employ critical theory to undress the influence of patriarchy on our modern world. In Zambia, from where I am writing, one of the practical ways we can do this is by questioning whether the patriarchal practice of *lobola* or bride-price (dowry) should be maintained or jettisoned in the interests of uprooting patriarchy in religion and society. The sooner we get rid of it, the more chance we have of two young people walking into marriage as equals.

References

Abraham, Kochurani (2019), *Persisting Patriarchy Intersectionalities, Negotiations, Subversions*, Cham: Palgrave Macmillan

Anti-Oppression Resource and Training Alliance [AORTA] (2017), "Challenging Patriarchy and Sexism Resource Packet," https://aorta.coop/portfolio_page/challenging-patriarchy-and-sexism/#:~:text=Below%20are%20some%20examples%20of%20how%20patriarchy%20man ifests%20institutionally%2Fsystemically,harassment%2C%20violence%2C%20and%20assa ult. (Accessed on 03.01.2021)

Bahlieda, Robert (2015), "Chapter 1: The Legacy of Patriarchy," *Counterpoints* 488: 15–67, Http://Www.Jstor.Org/Stable/45136330 (Accessed 02.01.2021)

Ferrari, Ettore (10 June 2019), "Women priests could help the Catholic Church restore its integrity. It's time to embrace them," *The Conversation*, https://theconversation.com/women-priests-could-help-the-catholic-church-restore-its-integrity-its-time-to-embrace-them-118115 (Accessed on 21.12.2020)

Fotopoulos, John and Aristotle Papanikolaou (19 June 2017), "Women and the Creed: "For us Humans and for our Salvation," *Public Orthodoxy*, https://publicorthodoxy.org/2017/06/19/women-and-the-creed-for-us-humans-and-for-our-salvation/ (Accessed on 03.01.2021)

Lerner, Gerda (1986), *The Creation of Patriarchy*, New York and oxford: Oxford University Press

Lyotard, Jean-François (1984), *The Postmodern Condition: A Report on Knowledge*, Minneapolis MN: University of Minnesota Press

Millett, Kate (2016), *Sexual Politics*, New York: Columbia University Press

Mukuka, Tarcisius (2021), The Man as Head of the House: The Peeing while Standing Hypothesis, Munich: GRIN Verlag, https://www.grin.com/document/983317

Napier, Wilfrid (6 October 2017), "Patriarchy is not the source of all evil," *The Southern Cross*, https://www.scross.co.za/2012/09/patriarchy-is-not-the-source-of-all-evil/ (Accessed on 02.01.2021)

Napikoski, Linda (24 January 2020), "Patriarchal Society According to Feminism," *ThoughtCo*, https://www.thoughtco.com/patriarchal-society-feminism-definition-3528978 (Accessed on 02.01.2021)

Omvedt Gail (1987), "Review: *The Origin of Patriarchy* [by Gerda Lerner], Economic and *Political Weekly* 22(44): WS70–WS72

About the Author

Tarcisius Mukuka is a biblical exegete by training. His ideal job is research in the Humanities and Social Sciences. He holds qualifications in Philosophy and Religious Studies (Diploma), Pastoral Theology and Counselling (Graduate Diploma), Licentiate in Biblical Exegesis (Masters) a doctorate in Biblical Hermeneutics. His doctoral dissertation was entitled "Orality as Casualty: Contextual and Postcolonial Analysis of Biblical Hermeneutics in *Bembaland*" (2014). He is currently a senior lecturer in Religious Studies Education at Kwame Nkrumah University in Kabwe. He is also President of Theologians against Violence. His research interests include postcolonialism and the Bible, gender and the Bible, the Bible and Misogyny, religion, politics and power. He is the author of Spoken Voice/Written Word: Negotiating How We Hear/Read the Bible (2016) published by Lambert Academic Publishing, *In the Eye of a Very Catholic Storm* (forthcoming), by Crown Arts Publishers, *Anatomy of an Episcopal Dressing Down and Clericalism: A Prince of the Catholic Church and an Ecclesial Irritant* (2020) and *Pope Francis on "Convivencia Civil" and a Movie called "Francesco:" Is there a Change in Catholic Church Teaching on Same-Sex Unions?* (2020) by GRIN Verlag.

Other Catholic Publications by GRIN Verlag by the Author

Mukuka, Tarcisius (2020), "Natural Evil, Suffering, a New Encyclical and a New World Order: A Socio-Religious Perspective on the Spirit of '*Fratelli Tutti*,'" Munich: GRIN Verlag

Mukuka, Tarcisius (2020), "On Fraternity and Social Friendship: Christian Life Community [CLC] and the Spirit of '*Fratelli Tutti*,'" Munich: GRIN Verlag

Mukuka, Tarcisius (2020), "The Catholic Church, Use of Hard Power and the Appointment of Bishops: The Case of a Fictitious but all too Familiar Scenario in *Zambezia*," Munich: GRIN Verlag

Mukuka, Tarcisius (2020), "Formation of Catholic Priests as Artisanal and not Policing: Pope Francis and the Formation of Catholic Priests for the 21st Century," Munich: GRIN Verlag

Mukuka, Tarcisius (2020), "Sexual Abuse in the Catholic Church across the Big Pond: The Vicar of Christ, His Nemesis and a Prince's Scarlet Cardinal Sins," Munich: GRIN Verlag

Mukuka, Tarcisius (2020), "Angels, Cherubim and Seraphim and Covid-19: Analogical Imagination or the Stuff of Nightmares?" Munich: GRIN Verlag

Mukuka, Tarcisius (2020), "Dirge to a Zambian Constitutional Amendment: When Religion Meets Politics," Munich: GRIN Verlag

Mukuka, Tarcisius (2020), "The Great Controversy Unplugged. Ideology of a Religious Classic," Munich: GRIN Verlag

Mukuka, Tarcisius (2020), "On calling anyone 'You Fool.' If Jesus did it, why can't we?" Munich: GRIN Verlag

Mukuka, Tarcisius (2020), "The expression 'Fratelli Tutti' from a Southern African Perspective: Contextualization from a 'Better Kind of Politics,' Munich: GRIN Verlag

Mukuka, Tarcisius (2020), "Anatomy of an Episcopal Dressing Down and Clericalism: A Prince of the Catholic Church and an Ecclesial Irritant," Munich: GRIN Verlag

Mukuka, Tarcisius (2020), "Pope Francis on 'Convivencia Civil' and a Movie called 'Francesco.' Is there a Change in Catholic Church Teaching on Same-Sex Unions?" Munich: GRIN Verlag

Endnotes

[1] An op-ed, short for "opposite the editorial page" is a written prose piece typically published by a newspaper or magazine which expresses the opinion of an author usually not affiliated with the publication's editorial board.

[2] BBC News (4 May 2007), "Chiluba's legacy to Zambia," http://news.bbc.co.uk/2/hi/africa/1715419.stm (Accessed on 03.01.2021)

[3] Wilfrid Napier (6 October 2017), "Patriarchy is not the source of all evil," *The Southern Cross*, https://www.scross.co.za/2012/09/patriarchy-is-not-the-source-of-all-evil/ (Accessed on 02.01.2021)

[4] *Ibid*

[5] *Ibid*

[6] Linda Napikoski (24 January 2020), "Patriarchal Society According to Feminism," *ThoughtCo*, https://www.thoughtco.com/patriarchal-society-feminism-definition-3528978 (Accessed on 02.01.2021)

[7] Tarcisius Mukuka (2021), The Man as Head of the House: The Peeing while Standing Hypothesis, Munich: GRIN Verlag, https://www.grin.com/document/983317

[8] Ettore Ferrari (10 June 2019), "Women priests could help the Catholic Church restore its integrity. It's time to embrace them," *The Conversation*, https://theconversation.com/women-priests-could-help-the-catholic-church-restore-its-integrity-its-time-to-embrace-them-118115 (Accessed on 21.12.2020)

[9] *Ibid*

[10] Anti-Oppression Resource and Training Alliance [AORTA] (2017), "Challenging Patriarchy and Sexism Resource Packet," https://aorta.coop/portfolio_page/challenging-patriarchy-and-sexism/#:~:text=Below%20are%20some%20examples%20of%20how%20patriarchy%20manifests%20institutionally%2Fsystemically,harassment%2C%20violence%2C%20and%20assault. (Accessed on 03.01.2021)

[11] *Ibid*

[12] John Fotopoulos and Aristotle Papanikolaou (19 June 2017), "Women and the Creed: "For us Humans and for our Salvation," Public Orthodoxy, https://publicorthodoxy.org/2017/06/19/women-and-the-creed-for-us-humans-and-for-our-salvation/ (Accessed on 03.01.2021)